Cover Your Six
Leadership

Other recent books by this author include

How to Quit Smoking in Only Three Days
Available on Amazon Kindle

The Seven Habits of Happily Retired People
Available hard copy or Amazon Kindle

Home Automation Made Easy
Hard copy or e-book

Build Your Own Free to Air Satellite TV System
Hard copy or e-book

Soon to be released in the *Dennis the Mentor*™ Series:

The Twenty-One Values of Real Men and Boys

DENNIS
the Mentor™

Cover Your Six Leadership

Dennis C. Brewer

First Edition

Printed in the United States of America

Copper Cove Publishing, Chassell, Michigan

ISBN-13: 978-0-9795559-3-0
ISBN-10:   0-9795559-3-0

About the Author

Dennis C. Brewer was born in Michigan's Upper Peninsula and is a graduate of Michigan Technological University. He holds a Bachelor of Science degree in Business Administration. Dennis is a veteran of military service to the United States of America, which includes enlisted service in the Navy and commissioned officer service in the Army Reserve and Michigan's Army National Guard. His varied career paths included experiences in military, state, and federal government; private enterprise; and his own technology consulting practice. Travel to Japan, Taiwan, China, Hong Kong, England, Canada, Germany, and the Philippines contribute to Dennis's world view and humanitarian perspectives. Dennis has many nationally published books and magazine articles included in his writing credits.

Dennis C. Brewer began learning about leadership at an early age. In Junior Army R.O.T.C training while in high school, he received many awards and medals over a four-year period. After high school, Dennis joined the Navy and quickly attained the rank of Chief Petty Officer (CPO) as one of the youngest CPOs in the Navy at that time. Like many of his highly motivated contemporaries, Dennis decided to become an officer and simultaneously joined the Michigan Army National Guard as an enlisted member and enrolled in Michigan Technological

University and the Senior Army R.O.T.C. program. Upon completion of his degree, Dennis was commissioned as a Second Lieutenant in the United States Army Reserve. After graduating with high academic honors from the Army Engineer Officer Basic Course at Fort Belvoir, VA, he returned to serve in the Michigan Army Guard, retiring as a Captain after assignments in many types of engineer units over twelve years, including recon officer, platoon leader, utilities engineer, and automation projects officer. One might say this immersion in leadership courses, coaching, and experience qualifies Captain Brewer with some degree of expertise on the topic of leadership, without taking into account his later remarkable careers in federal and state government, and in his own consulting practice.

Contents

About the Dennis the Mentor™ Series

Ten points about this series and its name.

1. In the publisher's view, everyone should have helpful mentors who can offer sage advice at important times on life's journey—all the way from a child's first communication to the end of life's journey.
2. Unfortunately, sufficient quantities of sagacious mentors are unavailable to everyone, so a book such as this can help fill the void.
3. The readily available mentors and would-be-mentors in any geographic area don't always offer the best advice and counsel.
4. Dysfunctional families, single-parent families, one-minute-parenting practices, less than stellar public and private educational institutions, and a shortage of true moral champions across society all lead to a shortage of suitable mentors.
5. The ideas, advice, and topical discussion in this series are offered up as one of many potential inputs for the reader to help them find their own solutions to problems or issues.

6. The information in each book is to be treated as simple advice from an author who is interested in these topics and has thought about them deeply enough to be willing to share his opinions in a natural and organized format.

7. The series recognizes that its typical reader is a very intelligent individual with some expertise of their own, but who wants to learn additional information and other points of view on the topics presented.

8. The texts are intended to offer insights to also help readers who haven't had the exposure to the topics or the opportunity to experience the subject matter themselves.

9. Mentors can be, if nothing else, entertaining, and so can a little book like this.

10. Anything you read can lead to new perceptions about yourself, the universe, and the people and things in that universe.

Prologue—Involved Leadership

I can't put my finger on the exact time or place, but I learned a long time ago that everything that happens in the universe follows a pattern or a group of interconnected patterns. The interactions are just like gears in a clock, one moving the other to reveal something we need to know or use. Sometimes, the patterns found in one field of study, such as biology, can be replicated in other fields of study in unlikely places, such as consumer buying habits. After getting an early introduction to the topic of leadership and spending most of my adult life as an action leader, thought leader, or advisor to others in a position to lead, I found and began using the pattern that successful leadership requires.

I respect what others have written about leadership, but I don't always share their points of view, particularly when they attempt to make the act and art of leadership sound complex. I disagree when they bring a reader to think leading is difficult. It is not. Other authors on the topic of leadership tend to fail to reduce leadership down to its most basic elements, leading you to believe that leading people is a difficult thing to do or too complicated to learn. When you do simplify the topic to find the most elemental patterns that give rise to all leadership qualities and techniques, you'll find that the six basic patterns presented here apply to leadership of self and others in all circumstances. If you or anyone else can learn, internalize, and act on these six simple core elements of leadership in your environment—whatever that may be—you can, indeed, learn to be a leader. This flies in the face of those who express that leadership can't be taught, that you must somehow be "born" with certain qualities that make you a leader. Regardless of how you think about this, the fact is that the best leaders in any environment are the ones who persistently display the six facets of leadership discussed in the rest of this book.

There is no need to make the subject of leadership complicated or only relegate leadership roles to the "experienced." School children, beginning in the third and fourth grade, can learn to lead others using the techniques in this text. Leadership simply requires consistently applying the six essential elements of leadership covered in this text.

There is no gender bias or delta in leadership ability: women and men who know and apply these principles can be equally successful at leading others in the workplace, home, clubs, churches, or any type of organization. Simply apply these techniques consistently and success can be yours. No cultural, ethnic, social status, or color bias exists when it comes to leadership. For example, General, then later Secretary of State, Colin Powell was respected as a leader by nearly everyone.

Leadership is a process that has little to do with title or positional authority. It involves taking action and getting others to move and work toward achieving your vision, your end-game place with you: pushing or pulling with you to move everyone toward the goal. The following flows to and influence flows from those who exhibit these leadership qualities, regardless of their position in the organization. You can take the lead wherever you find yourself in an organization or group by acting on the principles presented here.

Please also note that these techniques are also the same ones you can use to take your own accomplishments to new places and new heights. You can change things in your own life for the better by, in effect, leading yourself to new goals and accomplishments by following these principles as directed at your inner self. In the final analysis, leadership is acting out these principles—one after the other—every time you need to move yourself or others to accomplish new goals and objectives.

If you are new to a leadership role, memorize these six fundamentals in a simplified form, and keep the list in your planner, on your desk, or pin it to your refrigerator at home. I have intentionally kept the rhetoric and write ups short to keep the information simple and applicable across all types of organizations involving human endeavors. These fundamentals apply to all individual and group undertakings, be they military and police, business, church, non-profit, public service, political, or private enterprise. Use the *Cover Your Six* principles of leadership and you can become the leader you've always wanted to be. In some cases, you become the leader even when you don't want the role. When a group or team loses its way, you can always relate the failure to one or more of the *Cover Your Six* principles being violated or left out of the equation. Regardless of how you attain your leadership role, you can rely on these principles to serve you and the group you intend to lead.

Enjoy the read and begin to embrace your potential for new levels of success as a leader.

Acknowledgments

Thanks to the many leaders I have had who have helped me develop as a leader of people. Early on at Calumet High School in Upper Michigan, there was Master Sargent Anderson, a great role model for the young Army R.O.T.C. cadets. While I trained at the Naval Reserve Training Center in Hancock, Michigan, a guiding voice was cheerfully provided by Navy Captain Harold Meese. My first sea tour aboard the USS *Prairie*, I was mentored into a leadership role by ICC Senior Chief Petty Officer Joel L. Albee, who provided a daily dose of wisdom and stellar example. These men were early examples of leadership in daily action. There were more, including Chief Petty Officer Jerry Yetzer, while I served on recruiting duty that were a great example of the wise old sailor who spoke with authority and conviction. There were many others along the way, during my twelve years as a junior officer in the Michigan Army National Guard, who provided brief examples of leadership—some good, excellent really—and others provided examples too awful to recount or name.

I have seen and served under good leaders and bad and used this experience to forge for you, the reader, the cover-your-six leadership principles that work no matter what. So thanks to those who helped by their good and bad examples in helping me confirm the ideas presented here for you.

I would like to thank my wife, Penny, for granting to me some of our time so that this project and many of my other writing projects can be completed.

Thank you also to Patricia Wallenburg of TypeWriting for a great job of layout and to Marcia Baker for editing.

Inform Everyone of the Vision

To lead people to new places and accomplishments, you must first be convinced that what you're asking people to do stands as a possible accomplishment. If you show any doubts, your task to lead is lost before it starts.

It's too much to ask people to follow you blindly, although some will, but only for a short while. You must, as a leader, tell people what you expect from them. I call this making *people informed of the vision*: not just taking the next hill, or overcoming the next obstacle, or meeting the next sales goal. Your people must know the whole program or end-game as it applies to them and the whole team. Tell them in sufficient detail what their work efforts should bring about. This doesn't mean to micromanage people. Quite the contrary, it means informing them sufficiently of the goal or goals, so if the opportunity arises for them to reach the end-game without any more input from you, they must know what achieved success looks like and feel totally empowered to act independently. By fully informing people about what the goals are, you

1

empower them to act independently and take charge of accomplishing their part of the mission.

In shaping the vision for people to know, qualitative issues come into play. In organizations speaking to these qualitative elements often involves articulating details of the goals in terms of mission, vision, and values. A success without the honor of following the organization's values damages the success in the short- and long-term. In the context of sharing the vision as a leader, you must answer these six interrogatives: who, what, where, when, why, and how. Once you have done this, you can begin to trust your people to act responsibly toward achieving the goals and objectives you outlined for them. Operatives should never wonder why they are being asked to do certain tasks. Everyone should know the points of interaction with others and the obvious dependencies. All the team members should know the manner and means to be used to accomplish the broader short- and long-term goals.

In larger organizations, you can't expect the company president to be able to articulate all the details to a person on the shop floor, but he must be able to speak to and share enough of the details in general terms to that person. That president must test to be sure that his central message hasn't been altered in any way by any layer in the organization. President Regan is famous for saying "trust but verify," a requirement in any larger organization. In smaller organizations, the concept still applies, but it's usually easier to accomplish.

Keep Everyone Focused on the Priorities

Not every goal can be reached in a short time. Some efforts take days, weeks, months, or even years. Not everyone in your charge is able to filter out the minutiae and stay focused on reaching the group's combined goal. You have to monitor the team progress enough to know when your people have slipped and let some efforts go off task. People aren't set-and-forget machines. Occasionally, you must again bring the focus back to the end product and what that looks like. Events and circumstances out of your control sometimes require a tweak or a major adjustment along the way. It's critical that you, as the leader, reconnect often enough and long enough to keep everyone on the team *focused on achieving the priority goals*. The maintain-focus element can't be delegated to others, even in the largest of organizations. As the leader, you must return to your following to reconnect the dots and remind everyone in your charge of the priority goals.

You might need to implement a set of meaningful metrics to measure progress toward the goals in larger organizations. When going for smaller objectives and in smaller organizations, the measurements can be less formalized, but they are still necessary to have in place for your benefit as the leader. When I say "meaningful metrics," they measure results, not effort. Way too much energy is wasted measuring effort, when what matters is the results of the efforts. This concept has been reinforced in my observations in every environment where I have been involved.

Never allow returning to focus sessions to become a complaint and condescending session. This isn't a time to criticize the team or individuals because they did something wrong. There's no place as a leader for you to be damning or haranguing those who will, ultimately, bring you to achieve the team's success. Simply restate the goals and objectives in a positive way, and then ask if obstacles are in the way of achieving the success that you, as the leader, can help to remove. Dealing with bona fide obstacles is the leader's responsibility through personal direct intervention or appropriate delegation, or by calling in outside assistance. Regardless of the circumstances, staying positive, and leaving emotion and anger out of the equation is critical to maintaining the group's focus.

Keep All Team Members Motivated to Do the Best Work Possible

Some people tend to respond differently to stimulus be it carrots or sticks. Therefore, the model of rewards and punishments can't be the main method to motivate your team members. A leader defines the goals and group's success in such a way that everyone involved has a feeling of personal investment in that success. Everyone involved must have some skin in the game, so to speak. Something must be in it for them, whether it's praise, cash, pride, a sense of accomplishment, publicity, accolades, respect, or a sense of belonging to a successful group.

True and lasting motivation can't be applied externally like a coat or a bandage. True motivation comes from within the individual. Your motivational communication to keep operatives motivated has to trip a trigger within the individuals involved and the challenge is that isn't always going to be the same trigger for everyone in the group. The more you know about your team members, the easier it is to shape the motivational theme. That said, doing nothing to maintain motivation is never a viable option. The fact is, if you have no ideas, you can ask the team or individual: "What would cause you to want to achieve x, y, and z?" Once you have the answer, mirror that information back to the extent of the reality of the circumstances you and the team are in. It's essential only to promise that motivational carrot if you have the power and means to deliver it.

If all else seems to fail or evade you, you can deliver your own rendition of this speech in the next paragraph.

> *"You are here. You are part of this team. Look inside yourself to find your reason for being here and making your contribution. The rest of the team and I are counting on you to deliver the best work product and effort you have inside you. Let it out, give it life, and let's get this done together."*

When it comes to maintaining motivation, little things matter—a compliment along the way, a simple thank you, or a statement of appreciation all serve to give the individuals in the team a sense of connection to the broader objectives and goals. Let your team know they are valued and appreciated. Invest the necessary time and energy needed to keep everyone motivated to do their best work.

Provision Your Team with All the Necessary Tools

Provisioning is the leader's job, not that they have to do it themselves, but the leader has to see to it that provisioning is done. Provisioning has two aspects: the first is equipment, tools, and materials; the second is knowledge, information, and training. Both aspects are of equal importance.

Soldiers can only go to war if the guns and butter are already in the battle theater. In a business, it's impossible to make widgets without raw materials and tools. In a non-profit, the phone, computers, and operational equipment and resources must be at the ready for the volunteers to act on the organization mission. The worst thing a leader can do is fail on the logistics front. It usually isn't that complicated, but it always requires maintaining timely delivery. The second half of this equation is being certain that the operatives have the necessary information, education, and knowledge to get the jobs done. Any deficiency has to be addressed in the early stages of an endeavor.

The leader is responsible for thinking the entire venture out from start-to-finish and recognizing what is needed on both aspects of provisioning. Complex projects might make it difficult to anticipate every need, so close monitoring and collecting feedback is important to stay ahead of the required delivery curve.

Part of the strategy in developing military leaders, particularly higher ranking officers, is to give them experience in as many facets of the organization as possible. This includes personnel, intelligence, operations, logistics, planning, communications, and training. If nothing else, this broad-based exposure gives military leaders insight into what it takes to get ready, able, and equipped soldiers in the theater of operations. The size of the organization and the complexity of the tasks you're going to lead will combine to determine the complexity of provisioning in your environment. *Complexity* means the number of details that need to be handled to make the completion of the tasks possible. Regardless of the complexity of the tasks and tools needed as the leader you have to take full responsibility for *provisioning the team with everything necessary for success.*

Keep Individual Team Members Delighted to Be a Part of the Team

Strife in the ranks and file must be eliminated, meaning problems—whatever they are—must be solved right away before the problems and issues begin to impact the whole team's performance. Grumbling, gossip, negativity, or mumblings of revolt have to be handled without offending the person or the other team members. Problems won't go away when a leader ignores them. Glitches and hitches and fears must be dealt with immediately. By "dealt with," I don't mean mitigated, I mean eliminated. If a problem with one unhappy individual can't be solved, sometimes the only recourse is to replace that individual. You can't get the best effort possible or needed from a disgruntled team member. Everyone on the team must feel *delighted to be there*, and to be working with you and the other team members.

Often problems outside the workplace are the cause of performance issues within the workplace. Sometimes, it can be personality or ego conflicts with team members.

Sometimes, a lack of vertical or horizontal communications gives rise to team performance issues. Interview those involved to find the source of the discontent. Once discovered, you have to find a way to deal with the problem that works for you, your team, and the individuals involved.

As far as operatives feeling involved, and being willing and highly participating members of the team, three frames of thinking exist. The first frame of thinking is the unhappy leading to under performance. The second frame of thinking is those who are happy enough to be doing what is expected of them. And, the third frame of thinking is those who are delighted to be there and are performing at peak capacity. This is that necessary "delighted to be there" level, where individuals give getting-to-the-goal all they have in them or all that's necessary to get their team to the goal. Your goal as the leader is to keep your team members in the second or third frame of thinking at all times. Perhaps the more difficult part of being a leader is maintaining that cohesion and enthusiasm in people who, by nature, can find a hundred things wrong at any time. If you can choose the team members, choose those who have the traits of being nice people and the trait of positive thinking. Everything else can be taught and mentored if you begin with people who are genuinely nice and have positive can-do attitudes. You can't make people nice or fix rash attitudes. People have to bring that potential for positive attitudes to the table.

Reward Everyone
for a Job Well Done

Rewards can range from a simple "thank you" for a job well done to cash bonuses or simply a day off with pay. What is appropriate depends on the circumstances and the relevant value of the tasks performed. Without taking this step, you're setting yourself up to be a flash-in-the-pan, one-time-only leader. Your team members don't have to like you or be your buddy or friend, but they do have to respect you. Each one has to know their efforts—no matter how big or small—are fully appreciated by you as their leader, as well as by the rest of the team.

A leader earns respect by respecting the people in the trenches who do the work with an appropriate reward for their successfully completed tasks. It's perfectly fine to ask people in the early stages of an undertaking about what type of rewards they prefer. You have to find an avenue to *reward everyone for a job well done.*

Rewards for success have to be handed out or awarded with no strings attached. Rewards are for a past successful performance. For short-time rewards, whatever they are, create equilibrium between leader and follower. In effect, the awards reset the performance scoreboard. The leader is neither owed anything from giving the reward nor can the leader simply expect a high performance again because, a week ago, the person or whole team was *rewarded for a job well done*. This is a process that must go on as long as the team or organization functions, there is work to be done, and people are there to do that work. Cash awards, promotions, medals, trophies, whatever is common to the organization. Rewarding people for good work is as important as any other task of leading. Where formal and tangible awards aren't possible and, even when they are, the intangible personal thank you's and displays of appreciation remain as important tasks the leader must pay attention to and do consistently. Rewarding must be done as a matter of equal importance to any other thing a leader does.

Epilogue

This text has presented the six action techniques that allow you to lead in any type organization. Feel free to use these techniques to get results with the people you need to lead. Use this information as a compass to chart your course for success in becoming a more effective leader.

Write your six leadership principles down and use them as your daily reference as you begin your personal quest to become the best possible leader you can be.

This is what a leader does; he keeps everyone on the team:

1. Informed—of the Vision
2. Focused—on the Priority
3. Motivated—to do the Best Work Possible
4. Provisioned—with All Necessary Tools
5. Delighted—to Be Here on the Team
6. Rewarded—for a Job Well Done

Do this consistently and you too can be a leader.

This almost seems too simple and yet these *cover your six leadership* patterns of leader behavior have provided true leaders with success for centuries. These techniques can be easily learned and used wherever you find a leadership vacuum.

There's no magic to leading people. You don't have to be born with some elusive leadership gene. Leadership merely requires you to behave and act in a certain way that gives others confidence that you know what needs to be done, what it takes to get the work done, and that their work for you will be recognized and rewarded in some way.